OWLETS

by Genevieve Nilsen

TABLE OF CONTENTS

tadpole books

OWLETS

What is this baby?

An owlet!

It lives in the forest.

nest

It stays in the nest.

feathers

It has feathers.

talon

It has talons.

beak

It has a beak.

It eats.

WORDS TO KNOW

beak

feathers

forest

nest

owlet

talons

INDEX

16